Dino Days

Coloring Book for little Beginners

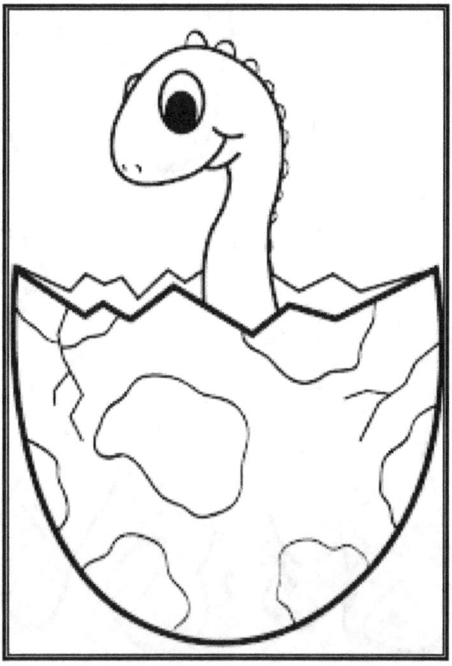

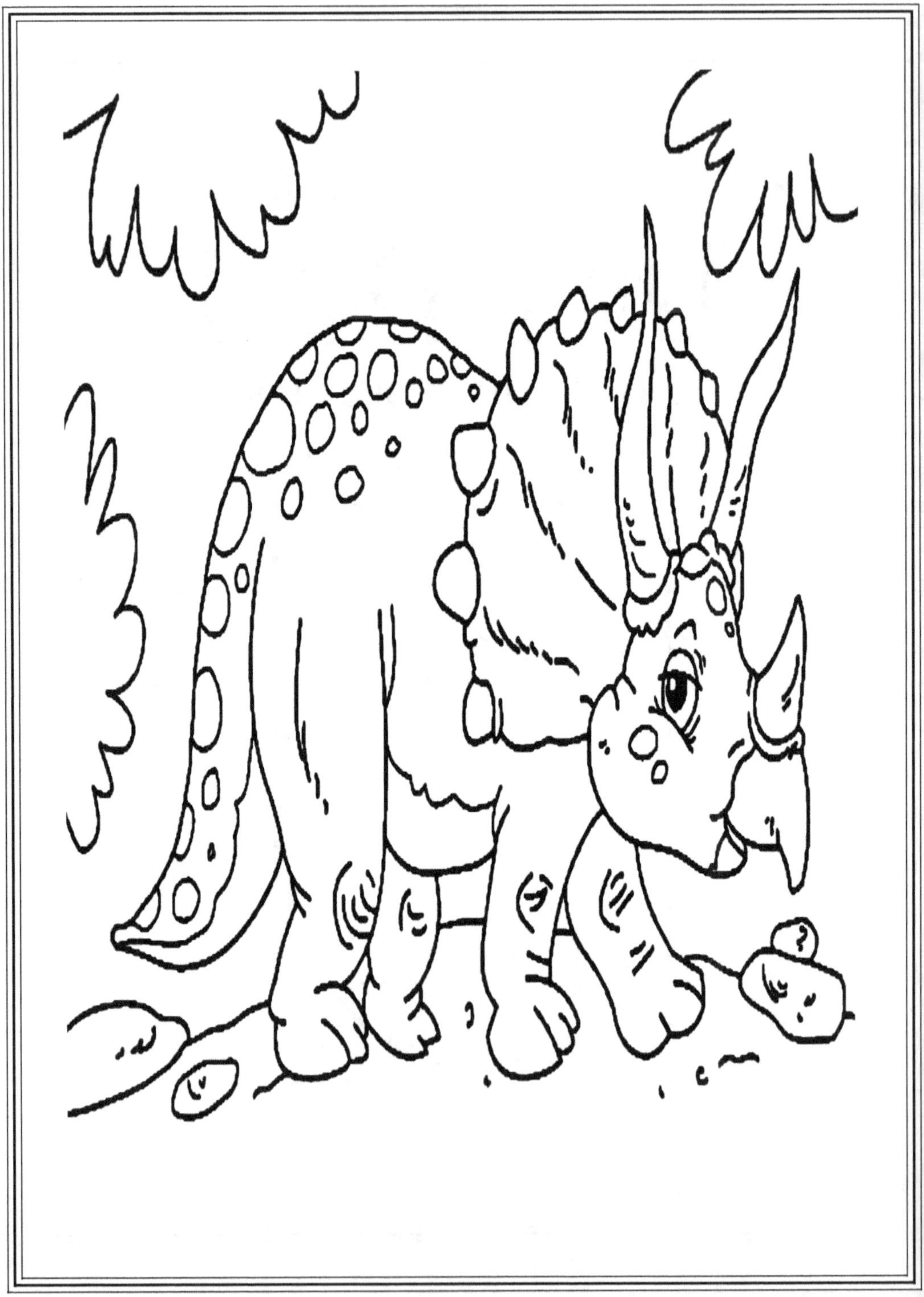

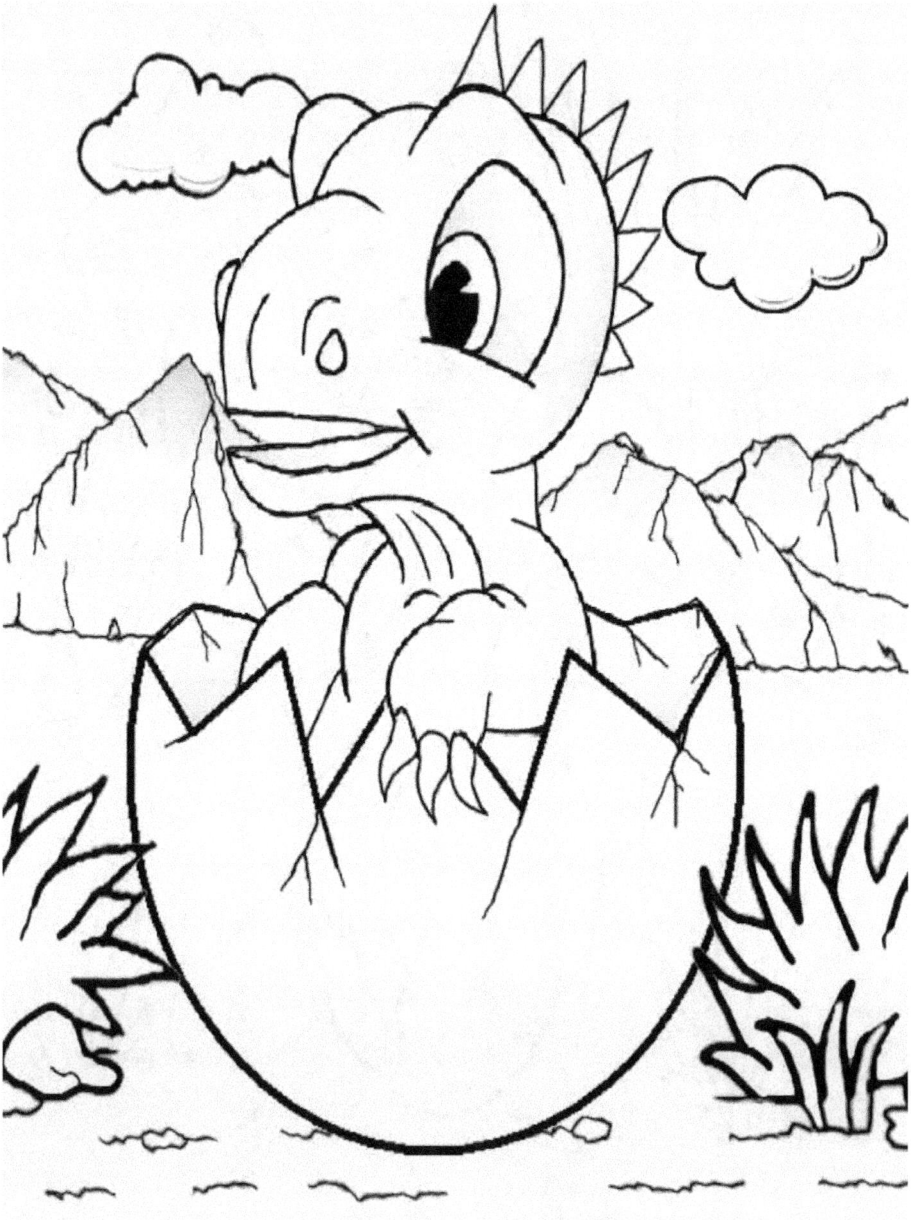

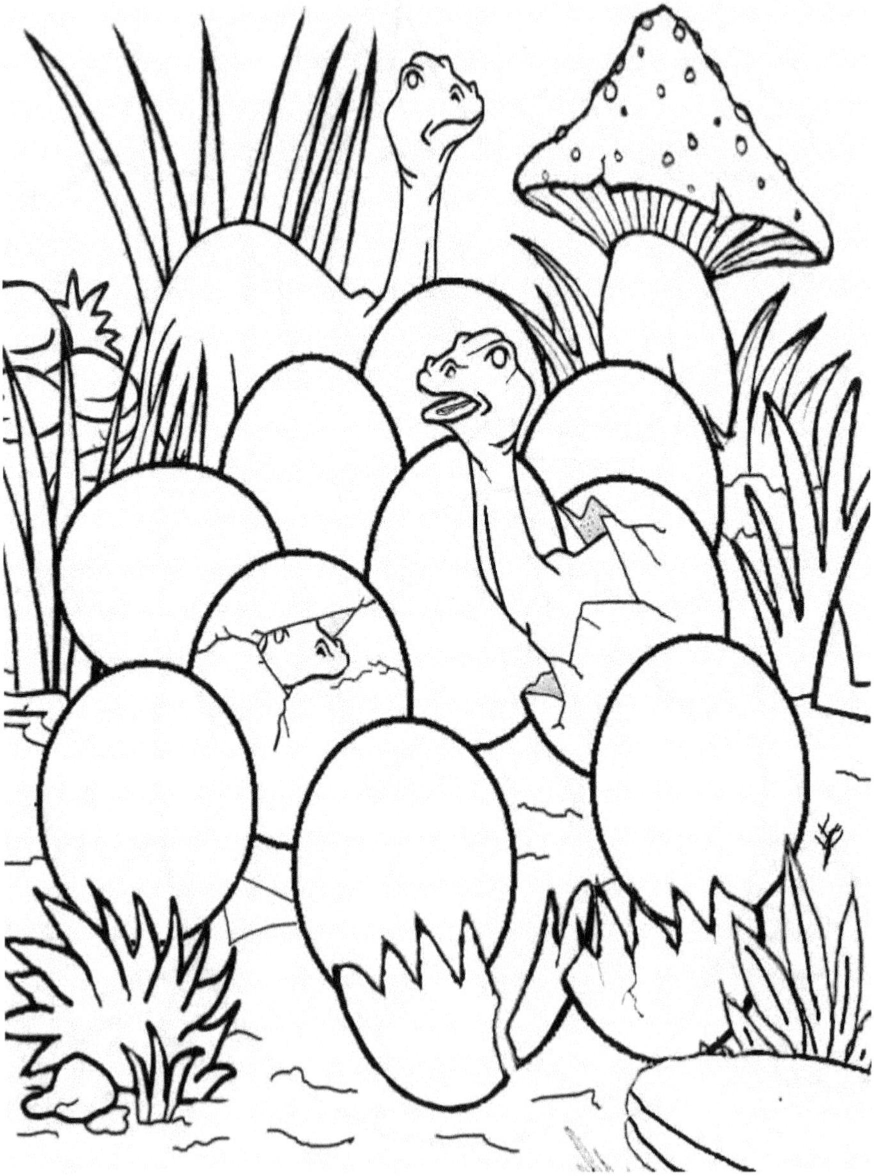

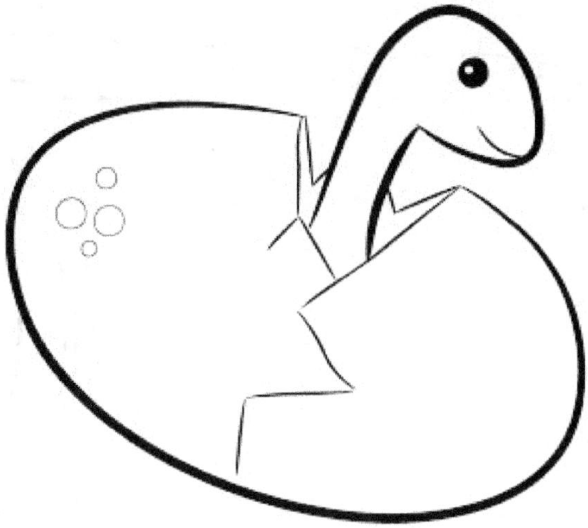
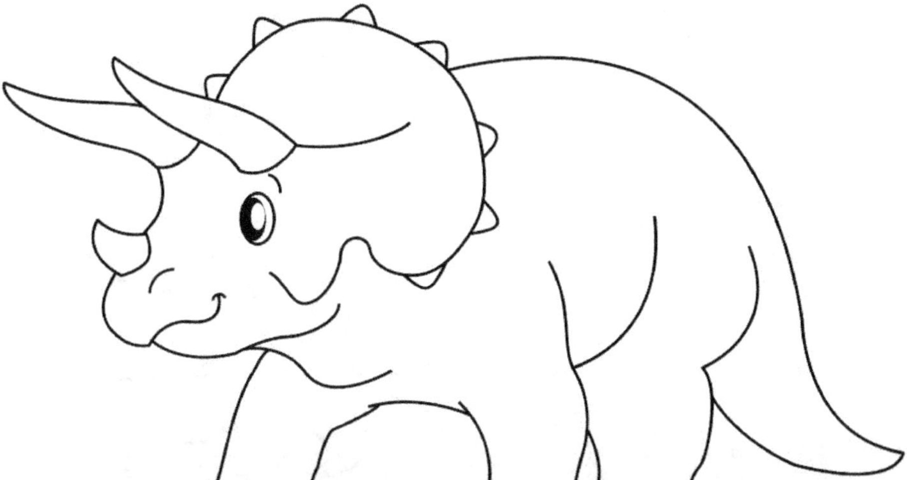

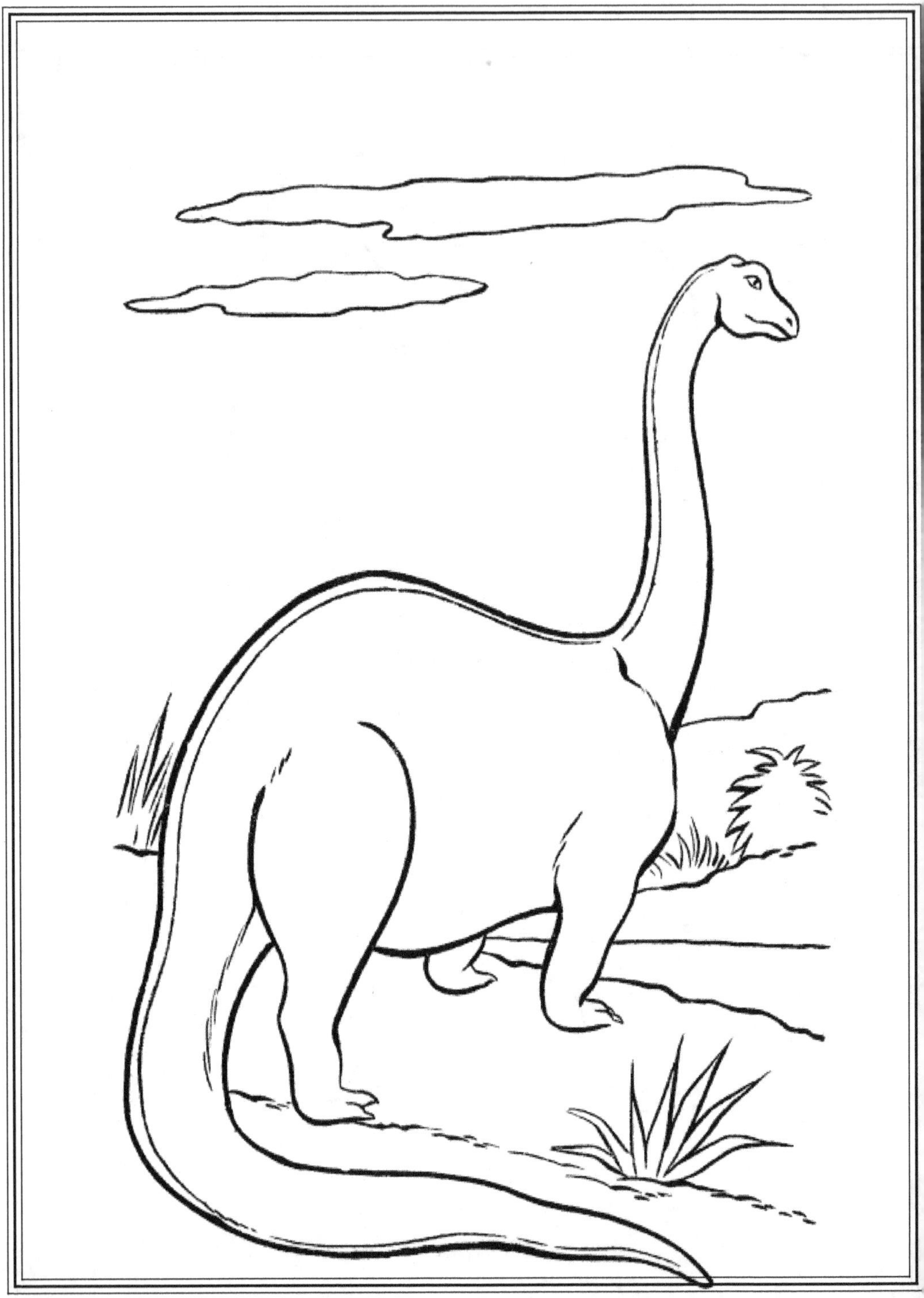

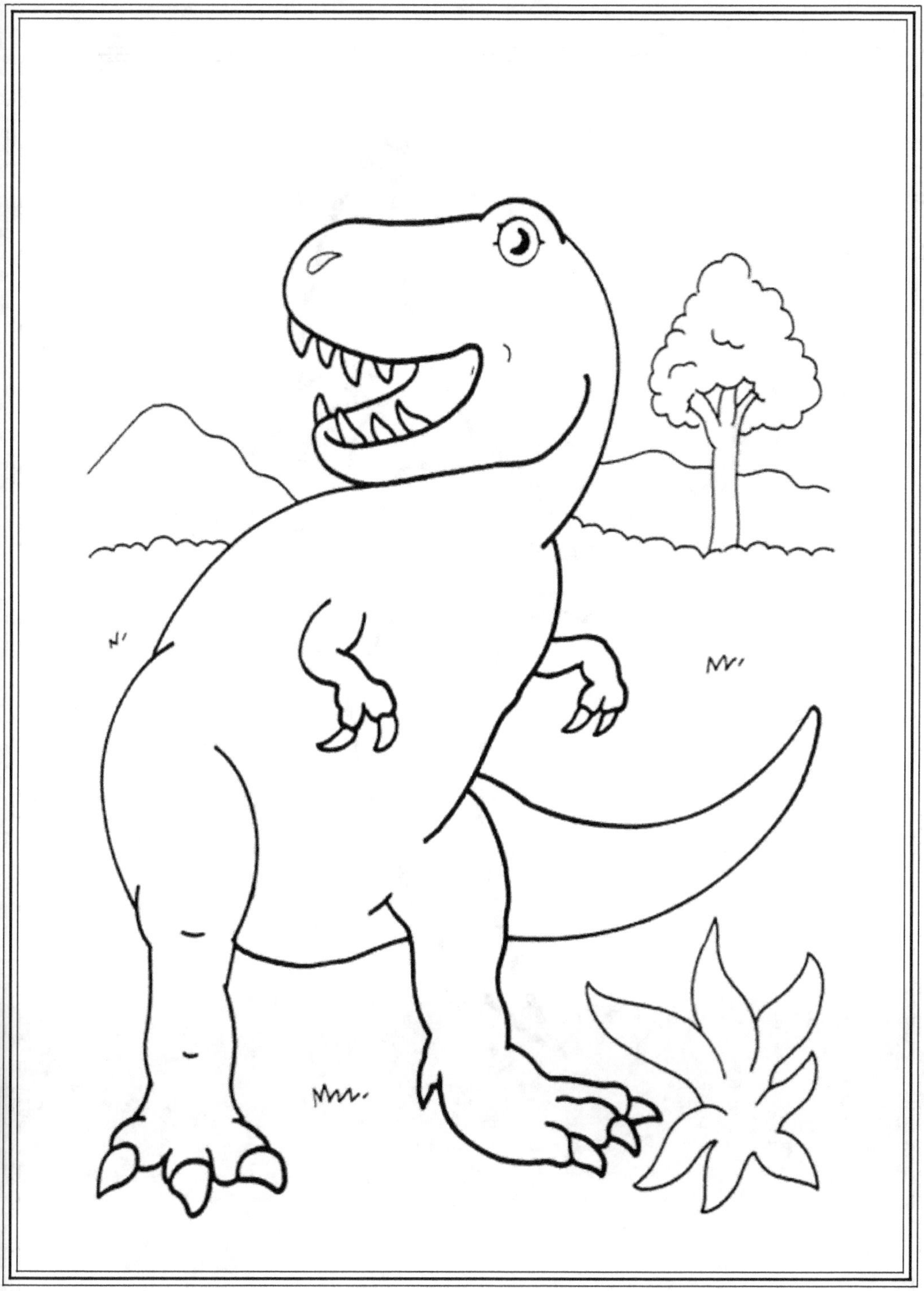

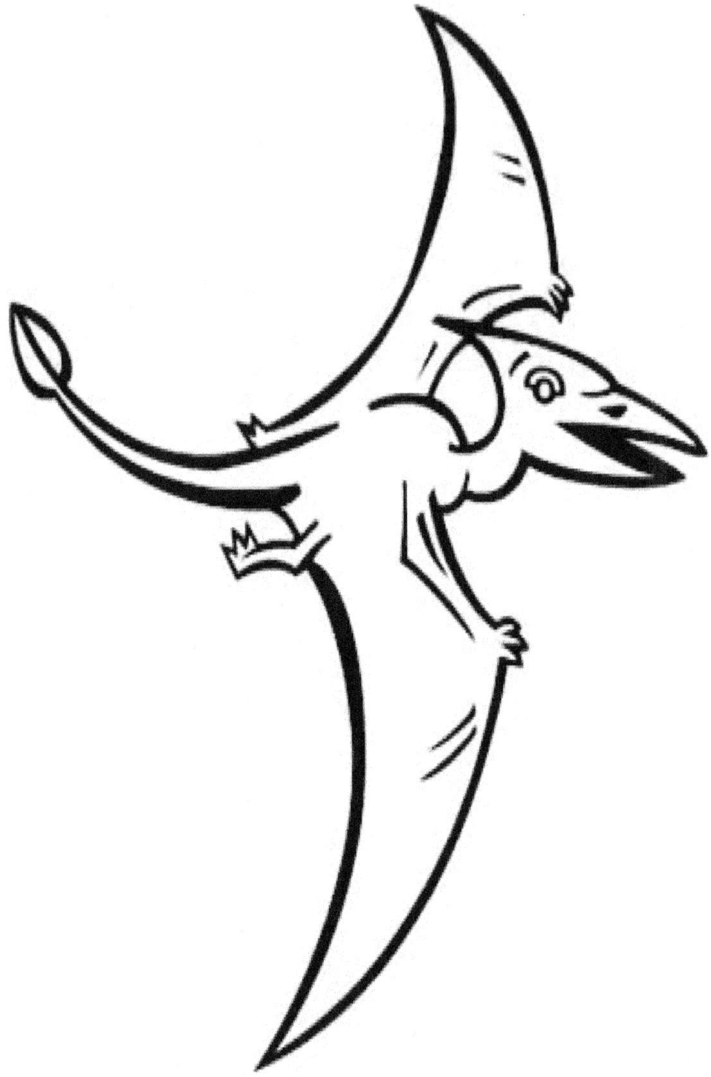

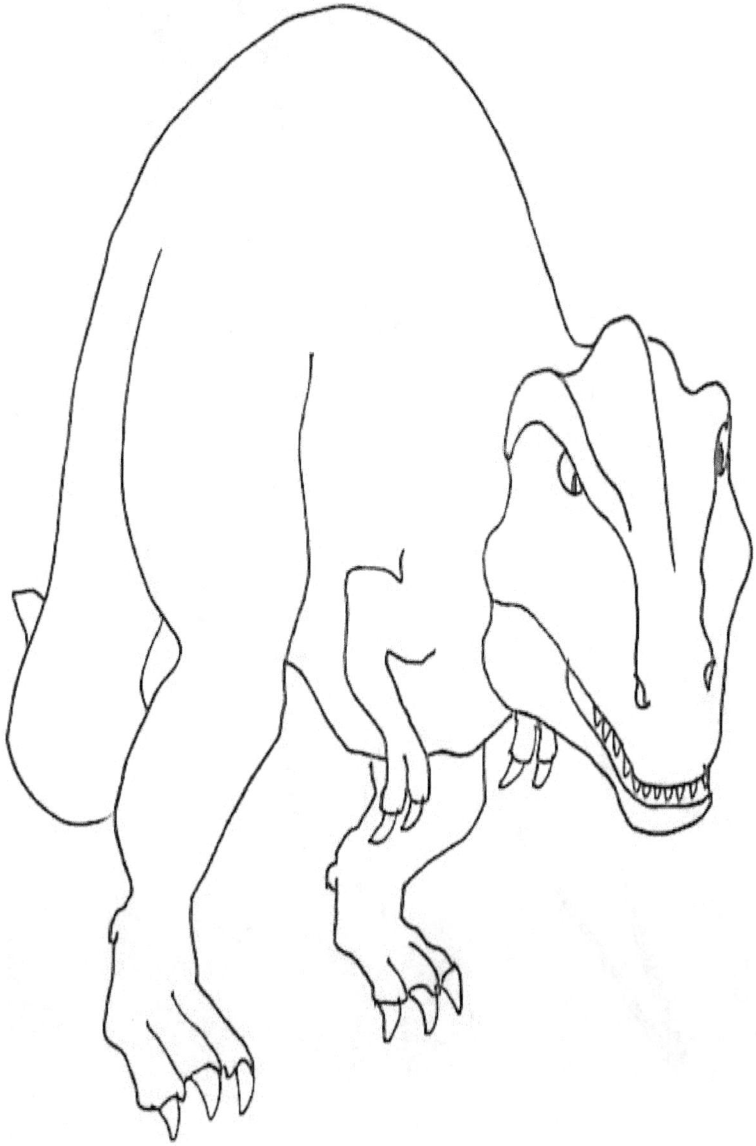

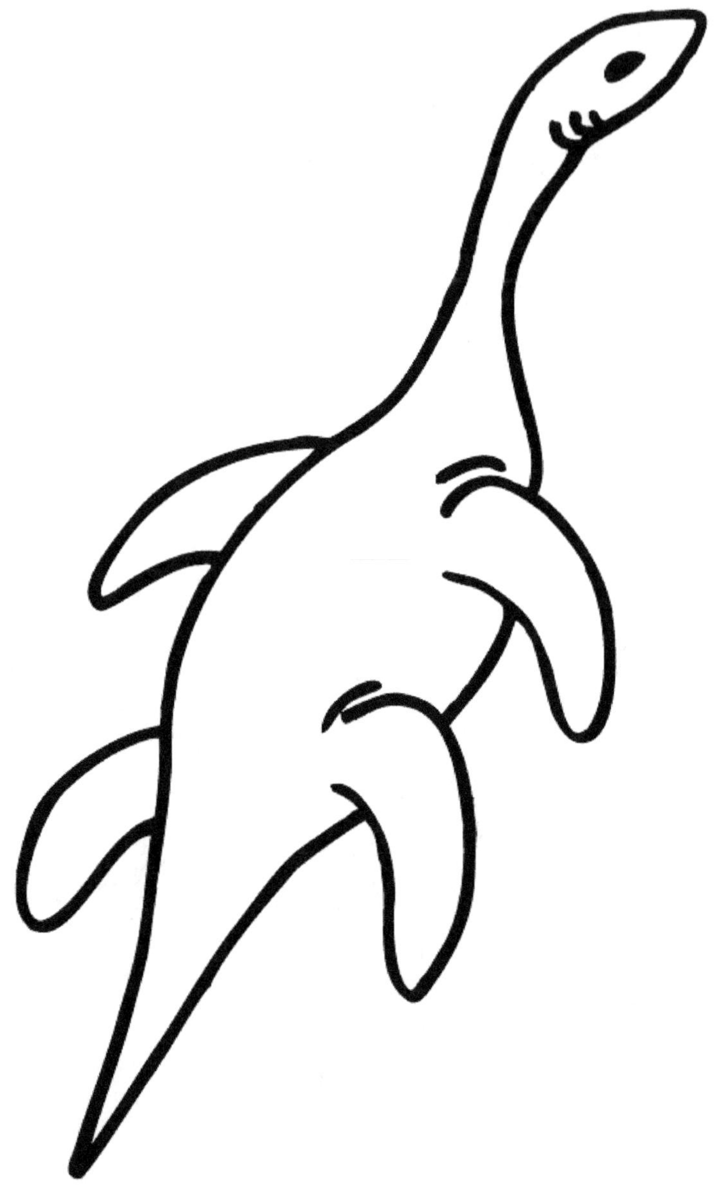

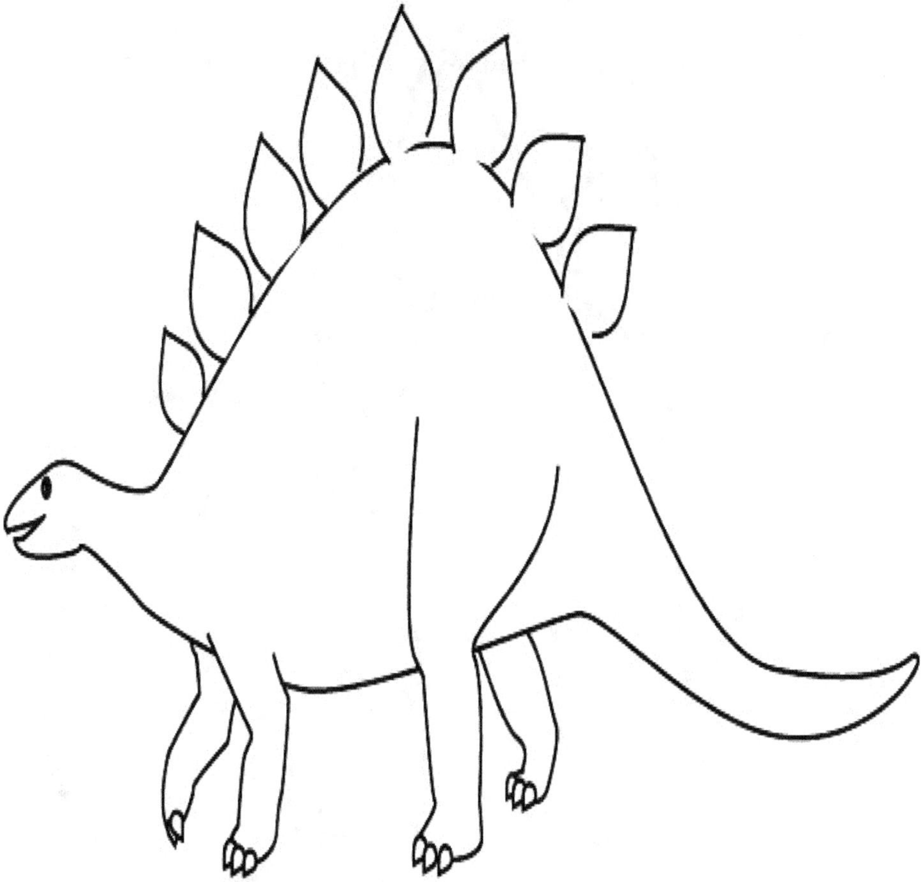

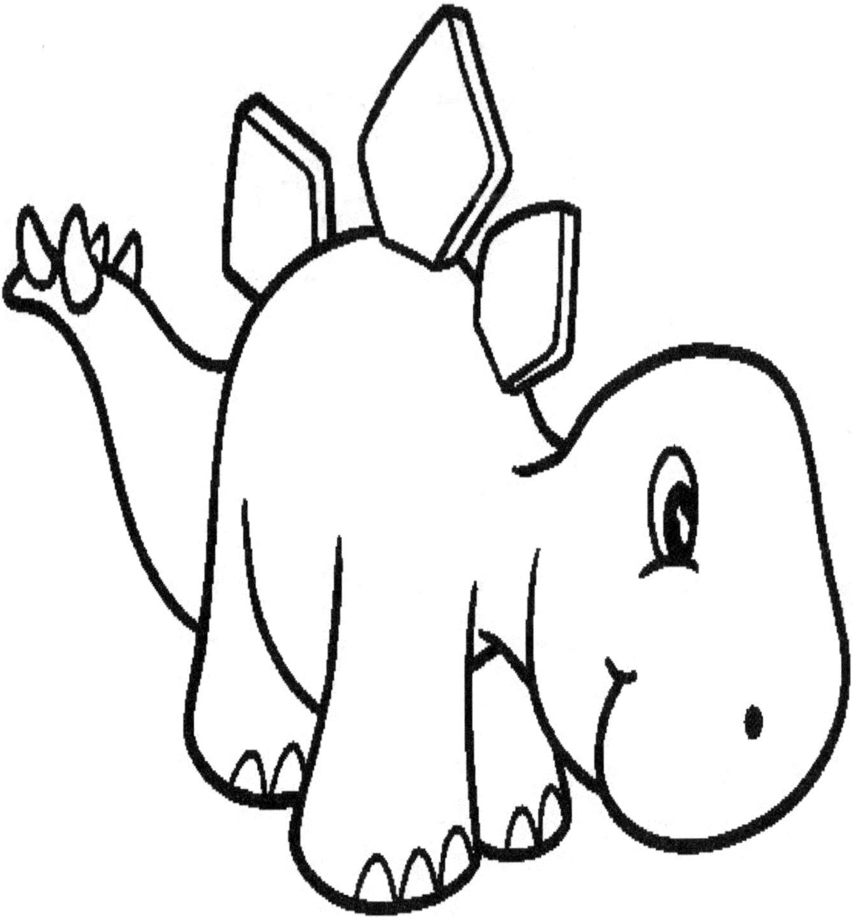

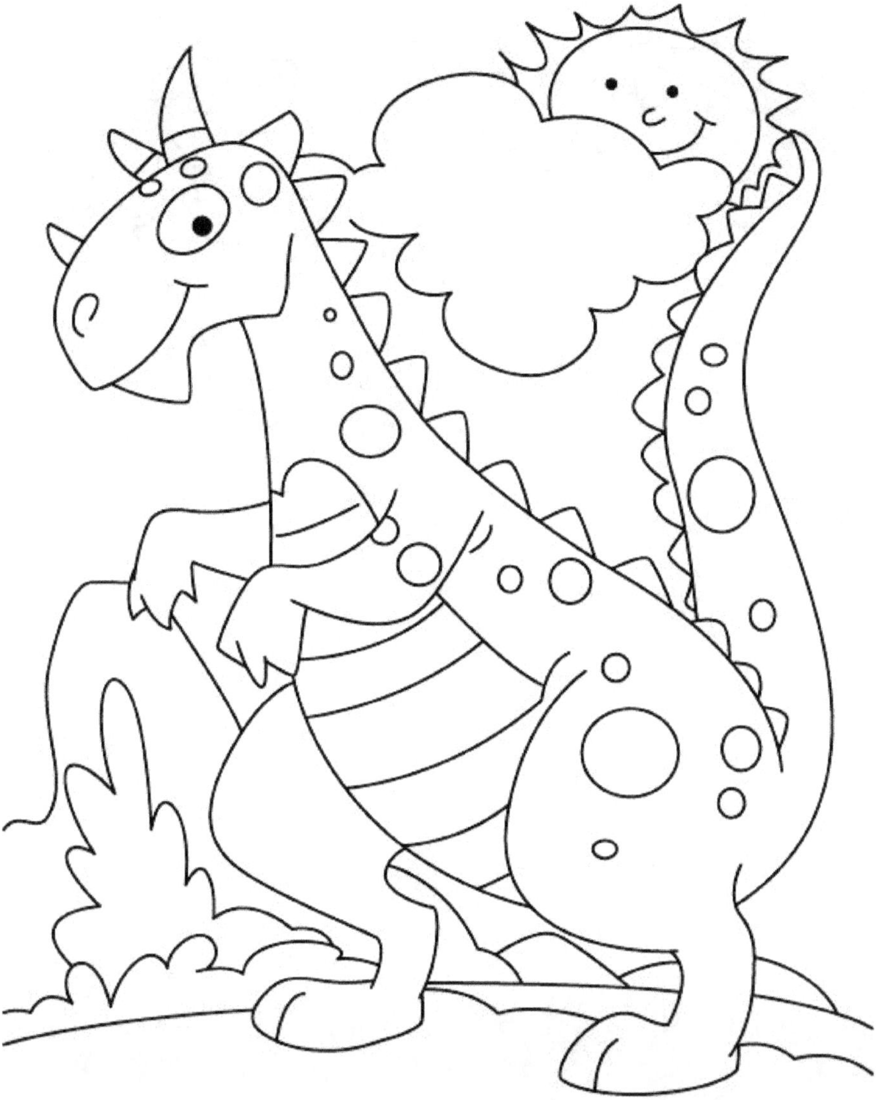

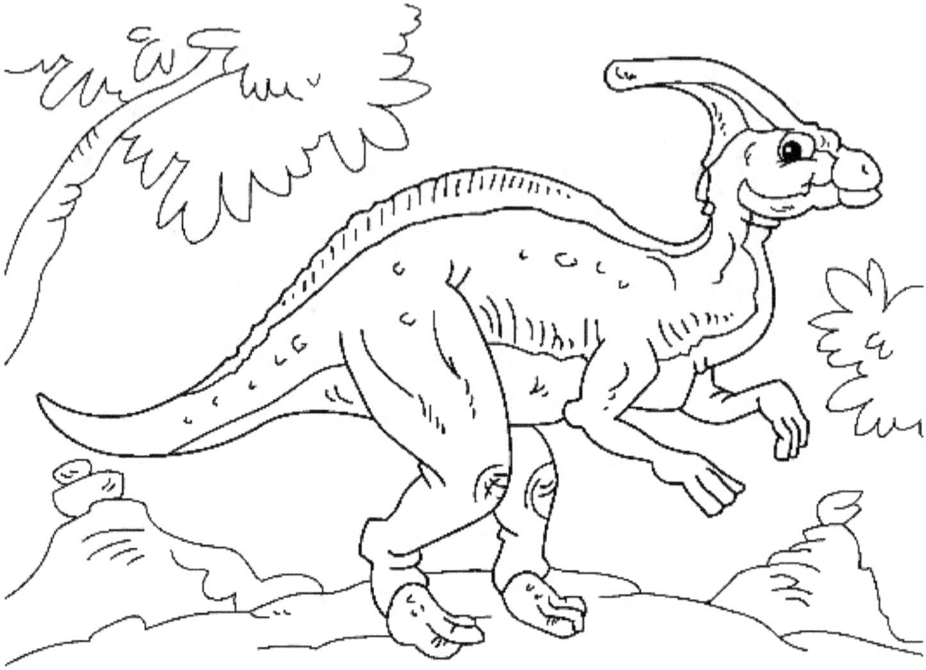

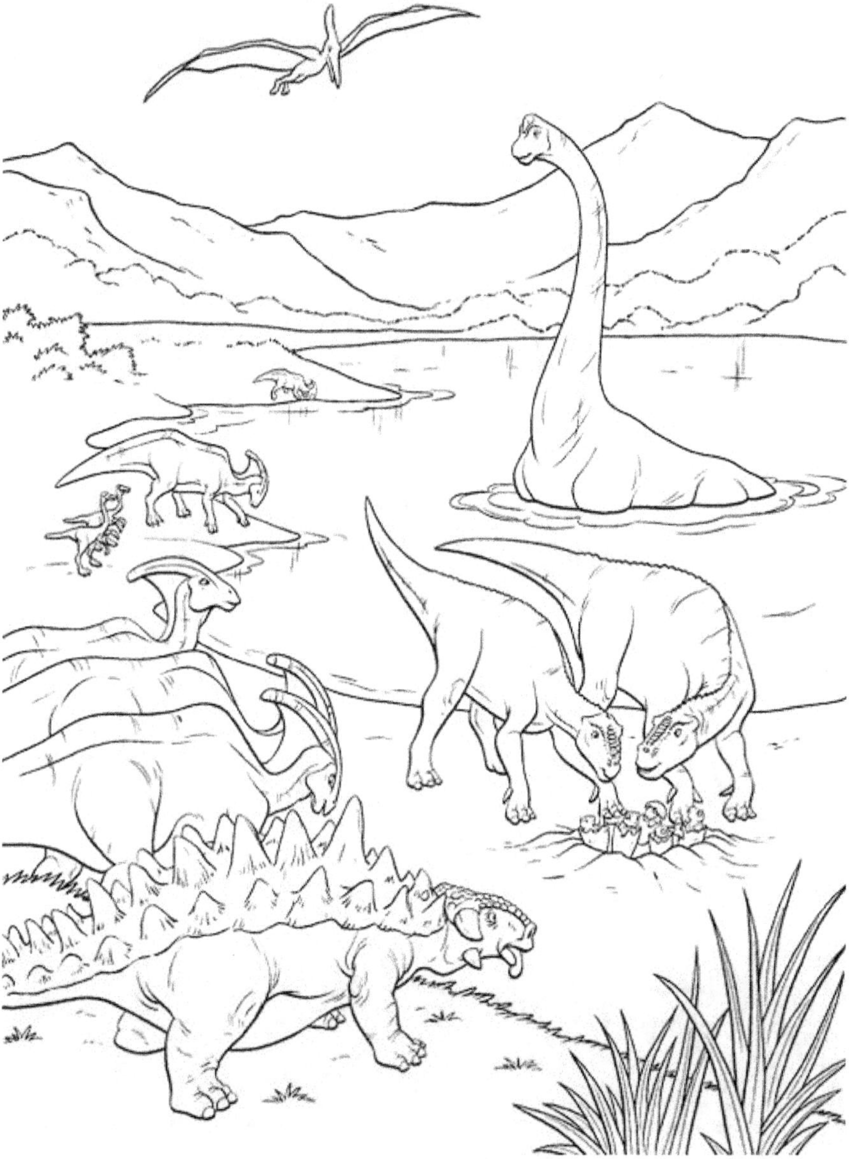

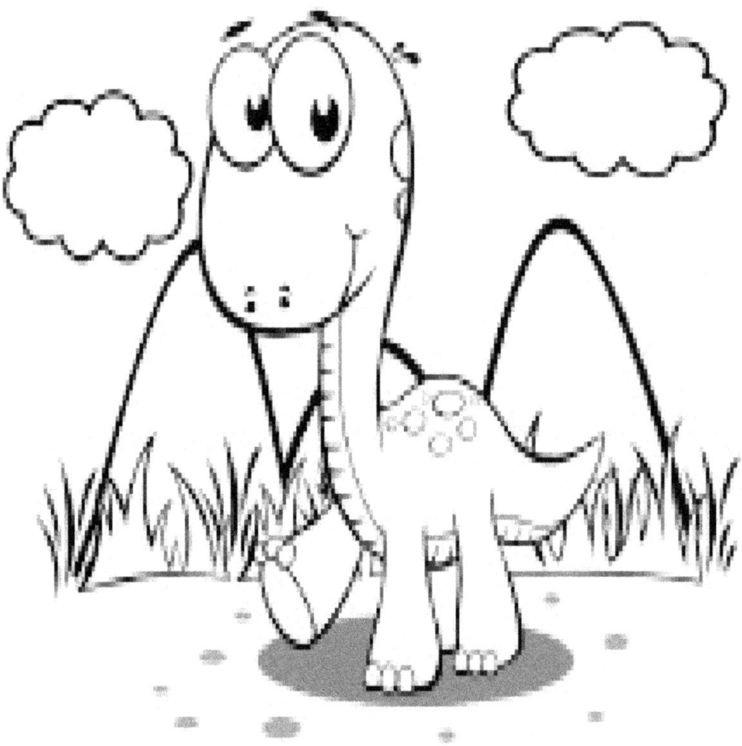

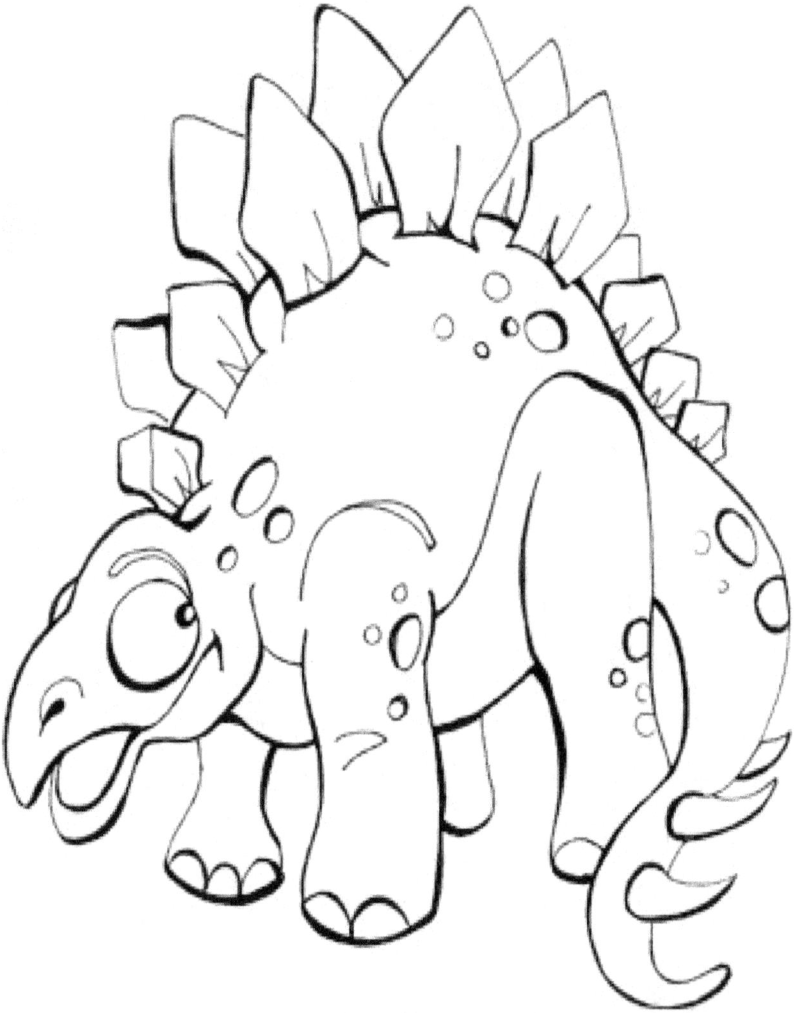

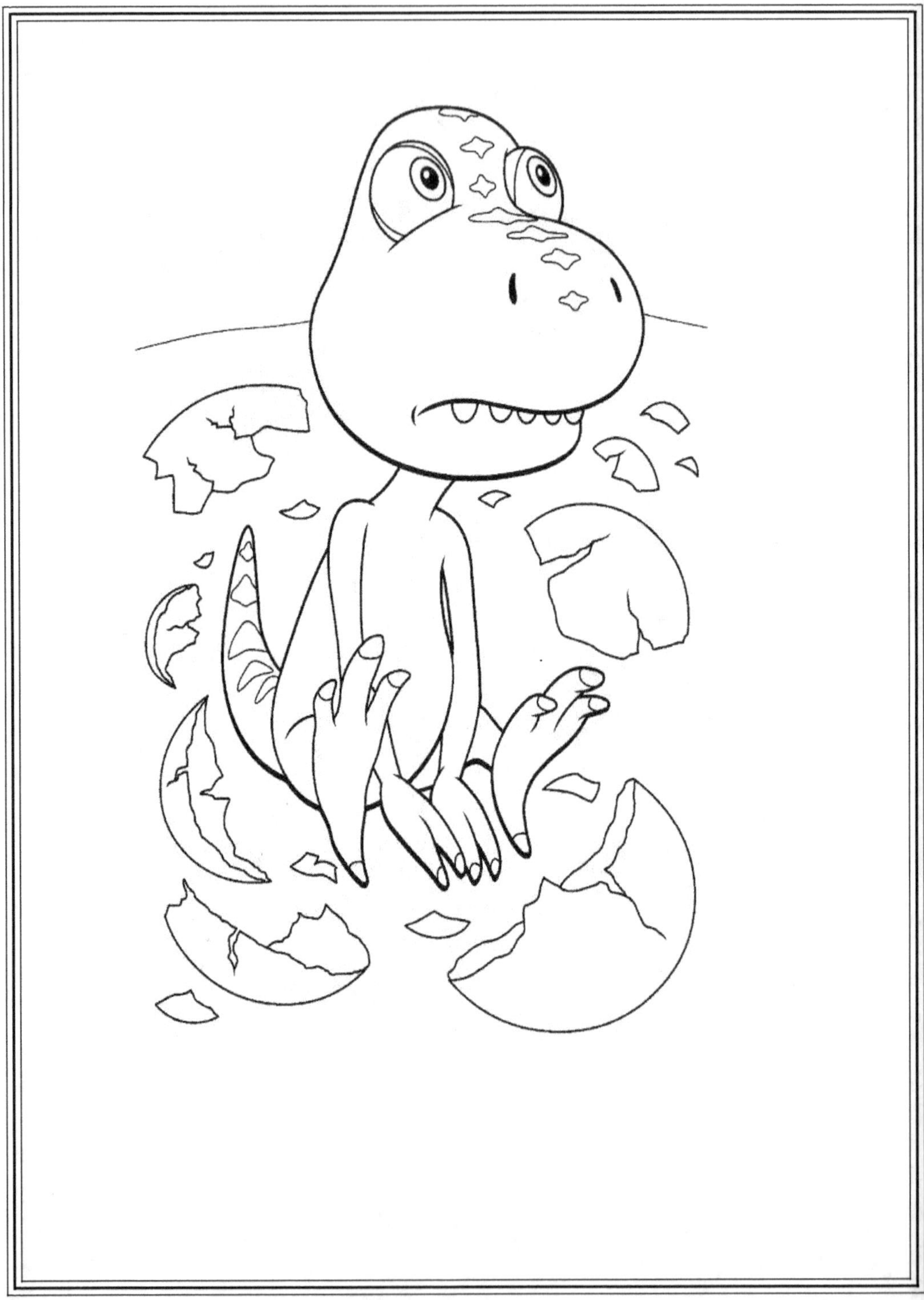

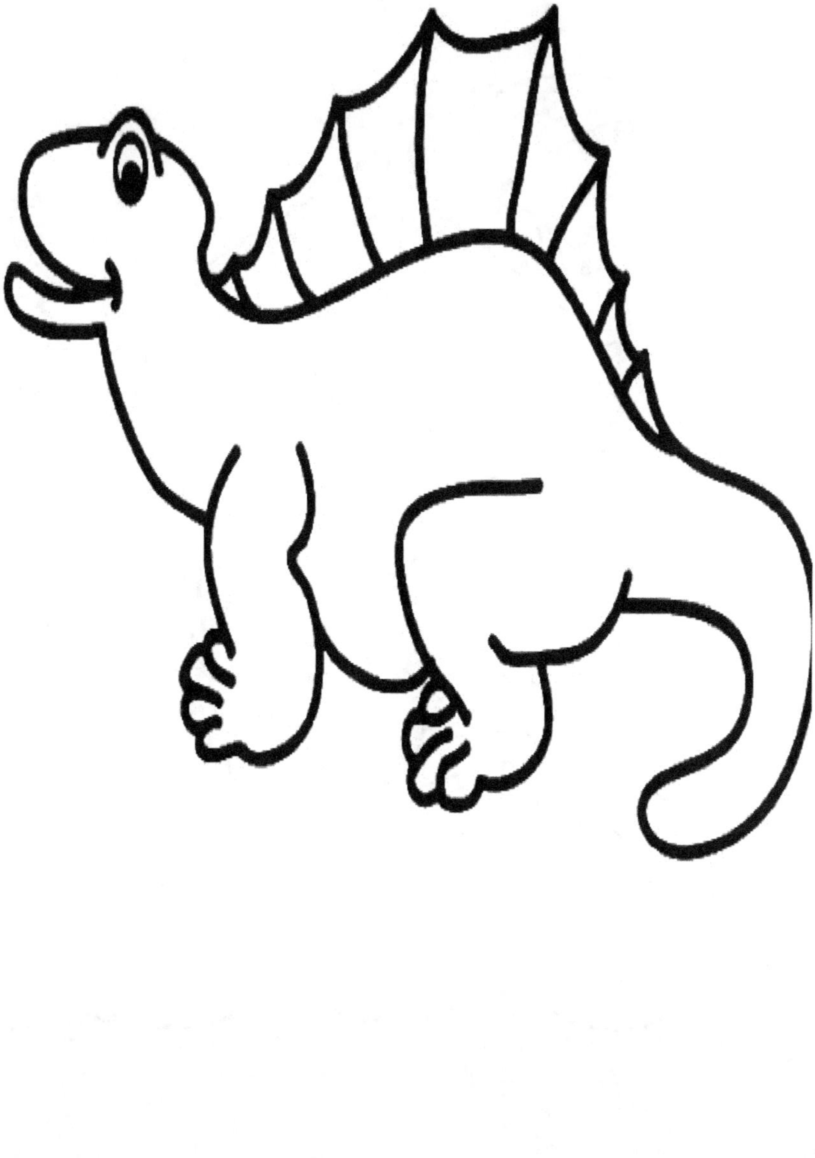

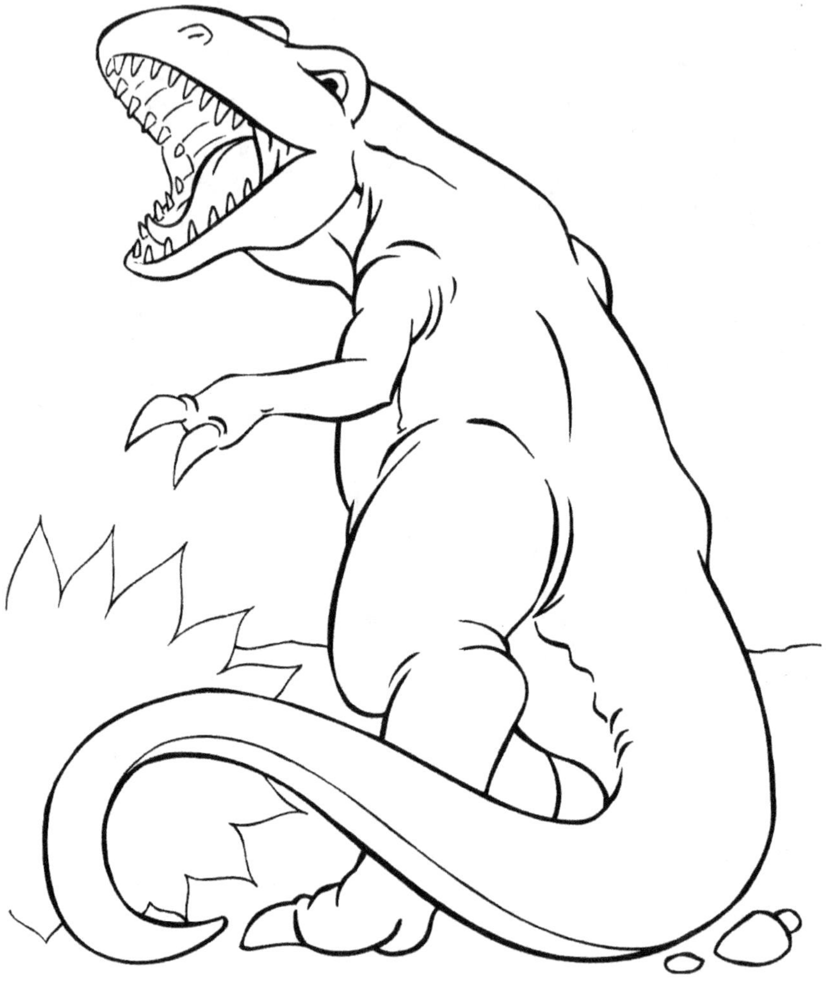

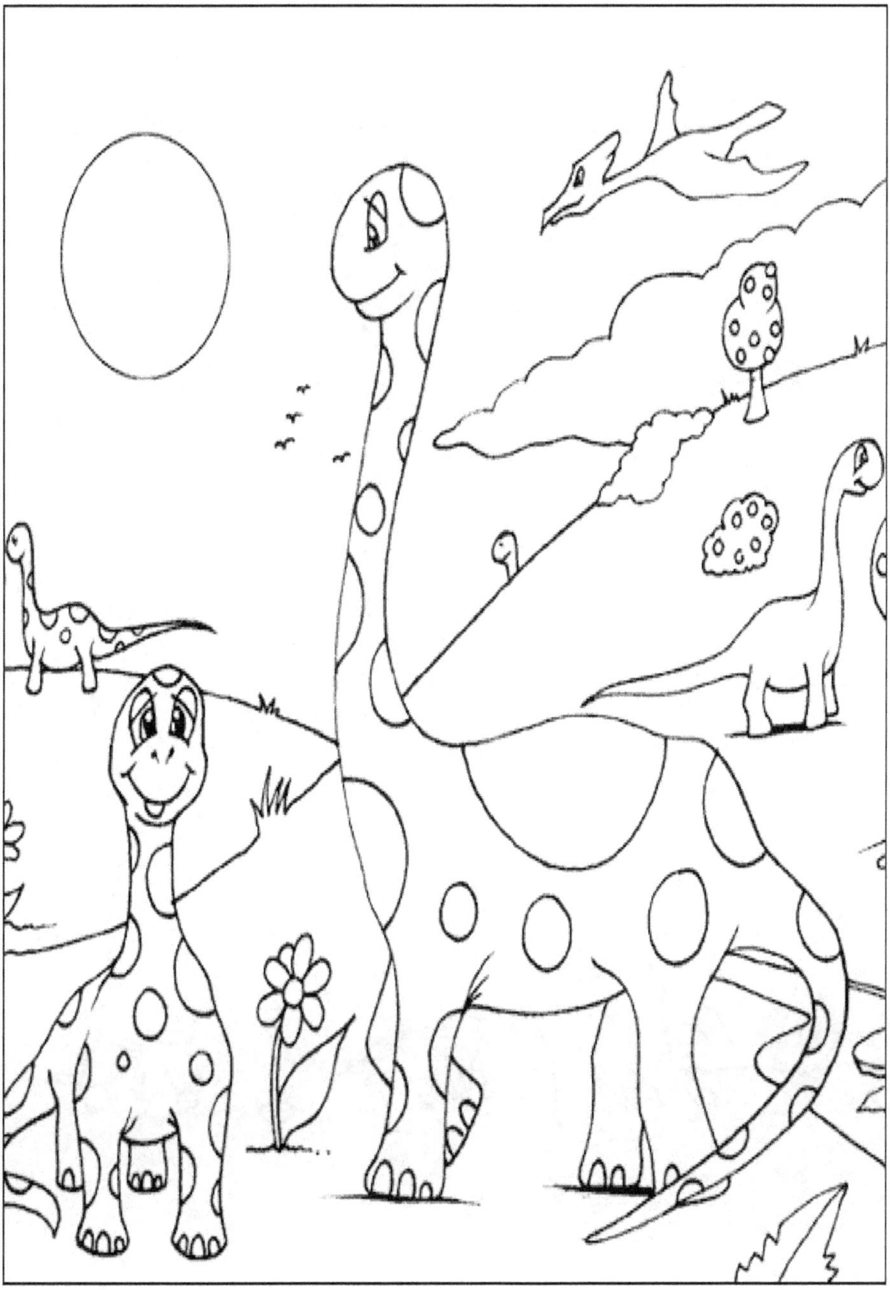

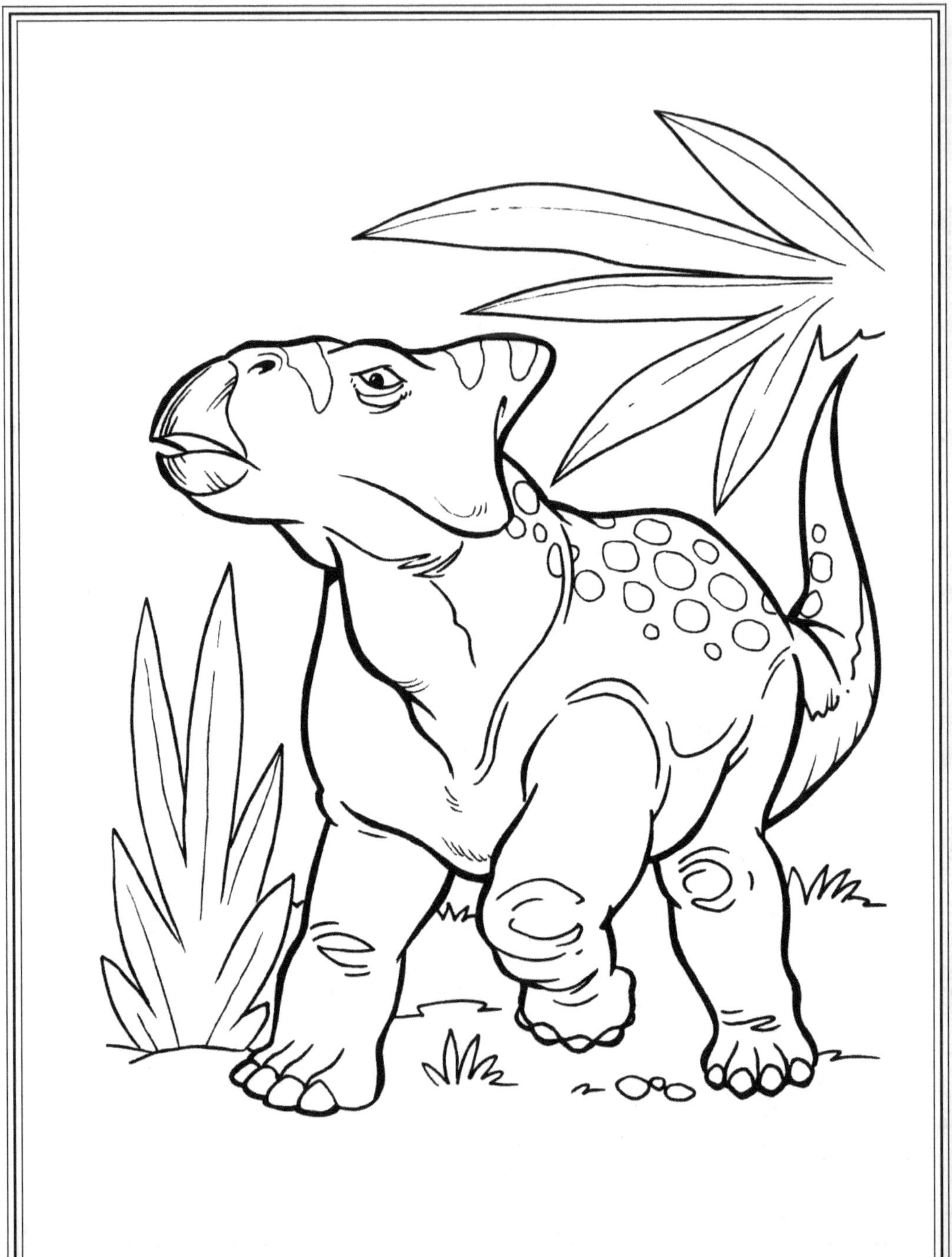

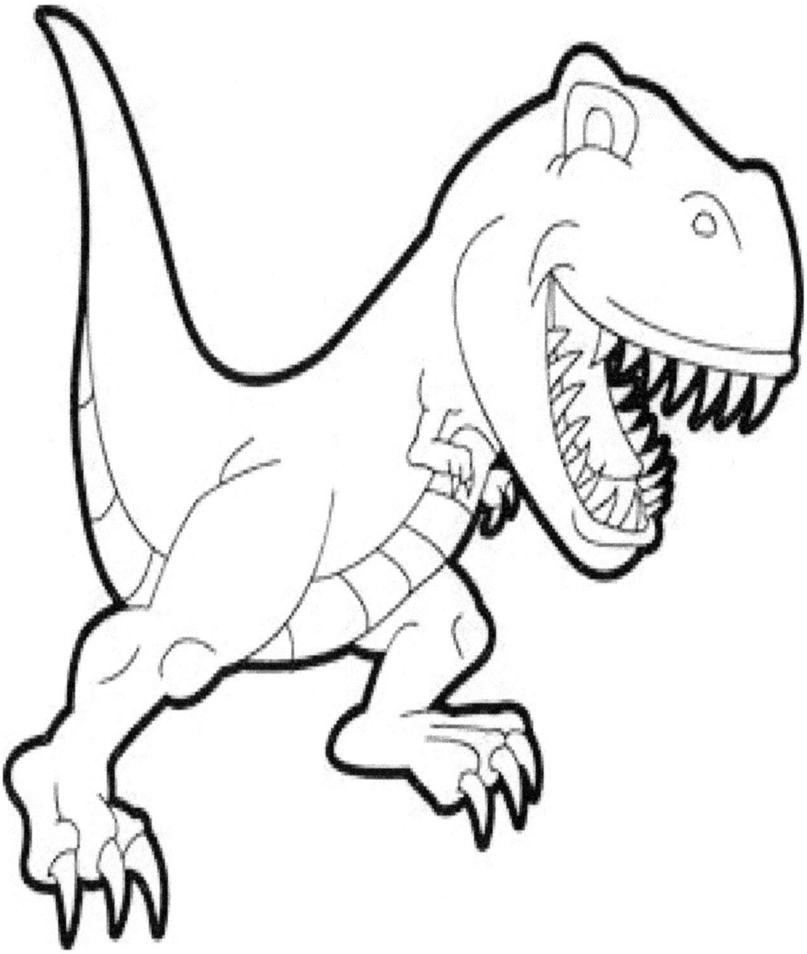

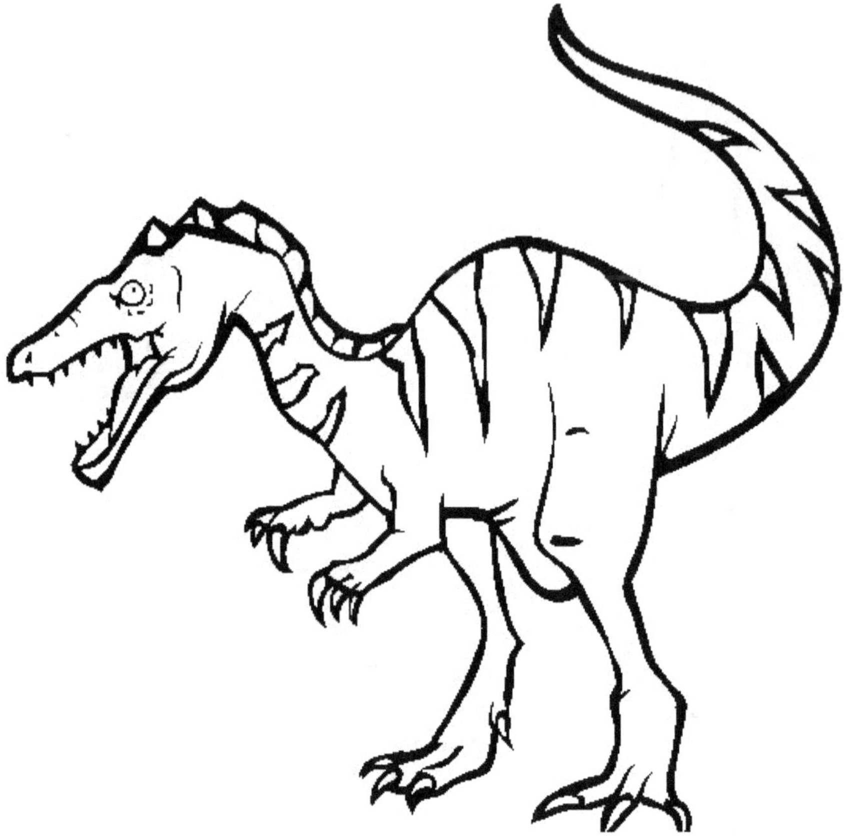

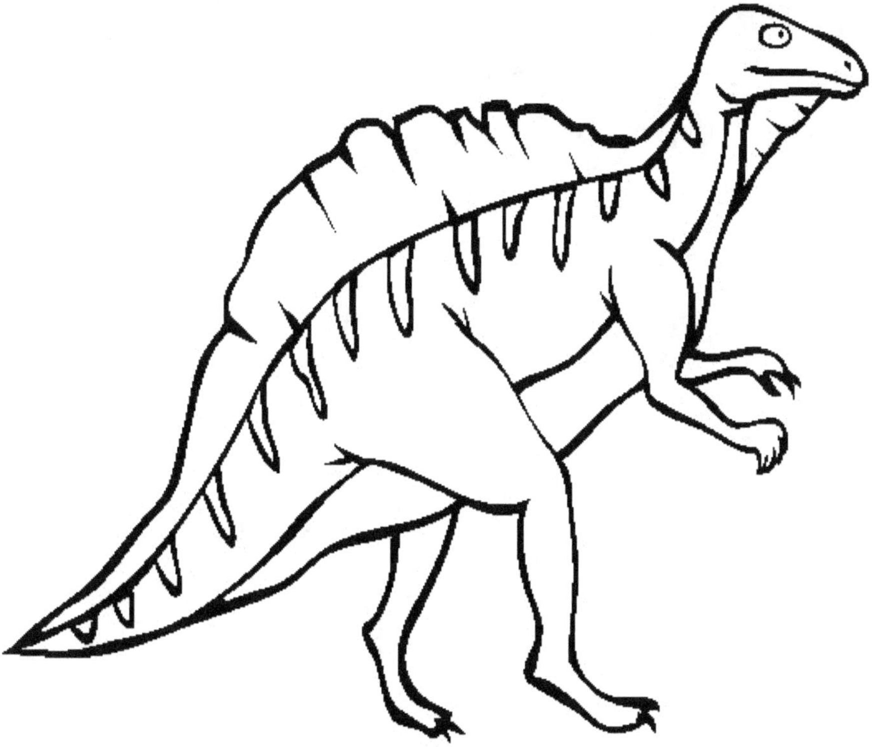

www.ingramcontent.com/pod-product-compliance
Lightning Source LLC
Chambersburg PA
CBHW070736180526
45167CB00004B/1781
* 9 7 8 1 5 4 2 9 1 9 2 3 4 *